OUTSIDE-THE-BOX

LATERAL THINKING

PUZZLES

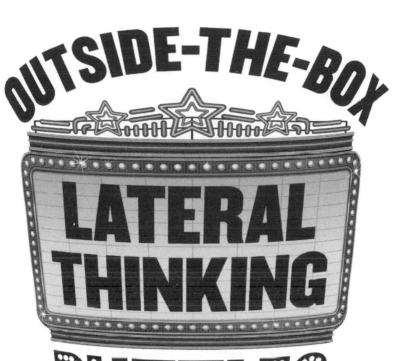

OUTSIDE-THE-BOX
LATERAL THINKING
PUZZLES

Paul Sloane & Des MacHale

PUZZLE
WRIGHT
PRESS

New York

PUZZLE WRIGHT PRESS

New York

An Imprint of Sterling Publishing
387 Park Avenue South
New York, NY 10016

ISBN 978-1-4549-0957-6

Distributed in Canada by Sterling Publishing
c/o Canadian Manda Group, 165 Dufferin Street
Toronto, Ontario, Canada M6K 3H6
Distributed in the United Kingdom by GMC Distribution Services
Castle Place, 166 High Street, Lewes, East Sussex, England BN7 1XU
Distributed in Australia by Capricorn Link (Australia) Pty. Ltd.
P.O. Box 704, Windsor, NSW 2756, Australia

For information about custom editions, special sales, and premium and
corporate purchases, please contact Sterling Special Sales
at 800-805-5489 or specialsales@sterlingpublishing.com.

Manufactured in the United States of America

2   4   6   8   10   9   7   5   3   1

www.puzzlewright.com

ACKNOWLEDGMENTS

Thanks to Peter McMahon for "A Simple Question,"
Lloyd King for "Legless" and "A Strange Creature,"
John Faben for "The False Confession," Felicia Nimue
Ackerman for "No Thanks," Jennifer Burdoo for "The
Ungrateful Hero," Francis Heaney for "Marked Man,"
and Norman Darmanin Demajo for "The Faulty Phone."
Jeremy Beadle's quizzes inspired the puzzles
"What a Mensch" and "Shoe Clue."

CONTENTS

....

Introduction 9

Puzzles 11

Lateral Thinking Animal Quiz 48

Clues 49

Lateral Thinking Geography
and Math Quiz 70

Answers 71

Quiz Answers 93

Index 94

....

INTRODUCTION

One of the most fascinating aspects of the human mind is our intense desire to solve problems. As little children we love riddles and puzzles. We take great delight in posing them and solving them. We progress to jigsaw puzzles, and there are few feelings more satisfying than pressing home the final piece of the puzzle. We graduate to crossword puzzles, sudoku, word puzzles, and the like. Some of us become scientists or philosophers and try to solve even more difficult puzzles: What are the stars made of? What is the meaning of life?

Many of the rest of us love to read or watch detective stories and try to figure out who committed the murder. We don't just want to be told; we want to figure it out for ourselves from hints and clues that the writers drop us. Education experts have realized that people much prefer to find things out for themselves than to be told. Good teachers have long known and used this approach.

Just as an athlete needs regular and sustained training for physical fitness, a thinker needs regular and sustained training for mental fitness. The best athletes enjoy their training and the best thinkers should enjoy their thinking exercises. One of the most enjoyable forms of training for mental fitness is lateral thinking.

Lateral thinking is clever thinking—thinking that sneaks up on you and surprises you with its simplicity. It often involves approaching problems from different points of view and finding the seeds of the solution in the problem. In this book we have once again assembled a collection of new and original challenges for you to pit your wits against. It does not matter if you are young or old, male or female, highly educated or unschooled. Your billions of active brain cells have the eager ability to work out what is going on. In each case we introduce a scenario to you, sometimes unlikely, sometimes contradictory, but underneath there is lurking a logical and usually simple explanation for you to find. The puzzles work best when one person, knowing the answer, presents the situations for one or more questioners to solve, but we've provided a section of hints for those of you who wish to try solving solo.

As authors we delight in pitting our wits against yours. So go on, improve your mental fitness with lateral thinking puzzles. You know it makes sense.

PUZZLES

Monkey Business

∙∙∙

A farmer had trouble with monkeys who came and ate the oranges in his orchard. What did he do to solve the problem?

Find clues on p. 50 and the answer on p. 72.

A Simple Question

∙∙∙

A policeman often asked people a simple question. The answer was obvious to any onlooker. Honest people gave the right answer but criminals often incriminated themselves by struggling to answer or giving the wrong answer. What was the question?

Find clues on p. 50 and the answer on p. 72.

The Job Doctor

A doctor does something for young people that does not improve their health but does improve their chances of getting a job. What is it?

Find clues on p. 50 and the answer on p. 72.

Wrong Note

In the middle of a rehearsal by a symphony orchestra a single note sounded out from the trombone. It was quite out of place. Why had it happened?

Find clues on p. 50 and the answer on p. 73.

In and Out

Every time his car stopped at a traffic light, Ronald would move to get out, then realize that he did not want to get out. What was going on?

Find clues on p. 50 and the answer on p. 73.

Ex-straw-dinary

When he used straw, many people were disappointed. Had he only used paper instead, those people would have been happy. Why did he use the straw?

Find clues on p. 51 and the answer on p. 73.

You Never Call

Alexander Graham Bell invented the phone but he never used it to call his mother or sister. Why not?

Find clues on p. 51 and the answer on p. 73.

Legless

Ricky lost one of his legs and he became very hard to please. Why?

Find clues on p. 51 and the answer on p. 73.

Disgruntlement

When the disgruntled workers joined in the celebrations they did not know they were starting a new tradition. What was it?

Find clues on p. 51 and the answer on p. 74.

Cut!

Why was an innocent television director arrested when he entered the U.S.A.?

Find clues on p. 52 and the answer on p. 74.

Flying Fish

Why did a woman throw a large fish across a room?

Find clues on p. 52 and the answer on p. 74.

All the World's a Stage

How did a very poor actor achieve his ambition of taking part in a Shakespearean play at Stratford–upon–Avon?

Find clues on p. 52 and the answer on p. 74.

Street Number

A man saw the word SIX written in large letters on a city street. What was he looking at?

Find clues on p. 52 and the answer on p. 74.

A Strange Creature

What living thing is a cross between a man and a cat?

Find clues on p. 52 and the answer on p. 74.

The Frame Game

Why did the curator of an art gallery remove a valuable painting from its frame?

Find clues on p. 53 and the answer on p. 75.

The Dopes

How was it discovered in 2006 that several Italian politicians were using illegal drugs?

Find clues on p. 53 and the answer on p. 75.

The Blooper

A terrorist bomber tried to escape from Britain but was caught at the very last moment by the police when he made a fatal error. What was it?

Find clues on p. 53 and the answer on p. 75.

Note This

In what team is harmony achieved as a result of extreme tension?

Find clues on p. 53 and the answer on p. 75.

Picture Perfect

A woman has no children but she carries a picture of two children with her whenever she travels. Why?

Find clues on p. 53 and the answer on p. 75.

Marked Man

A man kept getting visible pencil marks on the chest of one of his shirts. He wore it approximately as often as his other shirts, but none of the other ones had the same problem. What was happening?

Find clues on p. 54 and the answer on p. 75.

The False Confession

A man confessed to a murder he did not commit. He received the death penalty and it was carried out. Why did he confess?

Find clues on p. 54 and the answer on p. 76.

Overdressed

It was a very warm day but George was wearing two suits, two shirts, two pairs of socks, an overcoat and a hat. Why?

Find clues on p. 54 and the answer on p. 76.

The Tattooed Man

Why did a man who did not like tattoos have elaborate tattoos put all over his body?

Find clues on p. 54 and the answer on p. 76.

The Knifing

A masked man plunged a knife into Sam's chest. Sam was in a very serious condition and nearly died. When he recovered he tracked down the masked man and thanked him. Why?

Find clues on p. 54 and the answer on p. 76.

Deceitful Action

Why did the District Attorney send an e-mail to a colleague saying that the suspect John Jones was prepared to make a deal and confess to the commission of a crime, when both the D.A. and the colleague knew that this was not true?

Find clues on p. 55 and the answer on p. 76.

Just Add Water

How did a shortage of clean water cause many houses to flood?

Find clues on p. 55 and the answer on p. 77.

Who's at the Door?

If Marjorie visited anyone on Saturday or Sunday she would ring the doorbell. If she visited anyone on a weekday, she would knock on the door. Why?

Find clues on p. 55 and the answer on p. 77.

Fire! What Fire?

A number of people were warned that the structure they were sitting in was about to be consumed by fire, yet none of them moved or took any evasive action though they were free to do so. Why?

Find clues on p. 55 and the answer on p. 77.

Flightless

Why was a group of men pushing an airplane along the ground when it was fueled, perfectly capable of flying, and on a level surface where it could take off?

Find clues on p. 55 and the answer on p. 78.

Lab of the Rising Sun

What did the Japanese grow in laboratories to keep the Chinese out?

Find clues on p. 56 and the answer on p. 78.

The Bunk Stunk

Why did a man rub horse manure into his bed?

Find clues on p. 56 and the answer on p. 78.

Stage Only

Why was one of the most successful plays of the 20th century never made into a film or adapted for television?

Find clues on p. 56 and the answer on p. 78.

The Weaker Sex?

Men have the smallest one there is while women have the biggest. What is it?

Find clues on p. 56 and the answer on p. 79.

Airport Visitor

A man drives to the airport every day but never catches a plane. He does not work at the airport and he is not interested in airplanes. What is he doing?

Find clues on p. 56 and the answer on p. 79.

Ad Home and Abroad

An advertising poster for detergent showed, in four comic-strip-style panels, a pair of dirty socks, a box of the detergent, a washing machine, and, in the last panel, a pair of clean socks. It worked very well in the U.S. and Europe but failed dismally in the Arab world. Why?

Find clues on p. 57 and the answer on p. 79.

The Quake Mistake

In the 1906 earthquake in San Francisco more people were killed by fires than by the earthquake. But what was the unexpected cause of many of the fires?

Find clues on p. 57 and the answer on p. 79.

Flower Power

Why did a man send a large bunch of flowers to a woman he did not know, had never met, and had no romantic interest in?

Find clues on p. 57 and the answer on p. 79.

The Returning Father

A man abandoned his wife and baby just after the baby was born. They did not see or hear from him for many years but then the man showed up for his child's 21st birthday party. Why?

Find clues on p. 57 and the answer on p. 79.

The Artful Solution

Graffiti artists were told they would be prosecuted if they painted graffiti on city walls. How did they get around this threat?

Find clues on p. 57 and the answer on p. 80.

The Rattler

The thing that was believed to have killed a mystery writer was later heard rattling. What was it?

Find clues on p. 58 and the answer on p. 80.

A Weighty Problem

A man made the rather obvious observation that the more objects you put in a container, the heavier it gets. As a result of having this insight, he became a multimillionaire. How come?

Find clues on p. 58 and the answer on p. 80.

The Fortunate Nephew

Edna had three nephews: Alec, Billy, and Cedric. She loved them all equally dearly and was a very fair person. When she died it was found that she had left all her money to Cedric. Why?

Find clues on p. 58 and the answer on p. 81.

Unnoticed

When the famous writers C.S. Lewis and Aldous Huxley died, their deaths received very little attention in the media. Why?

Find clues on p. 58 and the answer on p. 81.

The Stranded Man

A man traveled to a town from his village by bus and spent almost all his money. Late that night he was stranded with not enough money for a taxi fare. All the buses had shut down for the night. He was too tired to walk the long distance and too scared to hitch a lift. How did he get home?

Find clues on p. 58 and the answer on p. 81.

Death of a Presenter

A woman whose job it was to present bunches of flowers to operatic sopranos and actresses after shows died of lung cancer. How did she get the disease?

Find clues on p. 59 and the answer on p. 81.

Shoe Clue

The actress Lotte Lenya claimed that when people met her, the first thing they did was look at her shoes. Why?

Find clues on p. 59 and the answer on p. 81.

Don't Look Now

Why was a woman walking down the street wearing a blindfold?

Find clues on p. 59 and the answer on p. 81.

Flat Out

A woman demanded that her husband give her as a Christmas present something that could go from 0 to 120 in three seconds flat. What did he give her?

Find clues on p. 59 and the answer on p. 81.

Initial Condition

Every time a man signs an official document, he uses a different middle initial. (John A. Doe, John B. Doe etc.) Why?

Find clues on p. 59 and the answer on p. 82.

Value for Money?

A charity gives small items to donors when they make a donation. They find that when they use cheaper, inferior-quality items they take in more money. Why?

Find clues on p. 60 and the answer on p. 82.

Cracking the Code

I faced a security door that had ten buttons. To gain entry I had to press three buttons in the correct order. There were 720 different permutations and I did not know the code. The door was locked and nobody told me the combination but I soon figured it out. How did I do it?

Find clues on p. 60 and the answer on p. 82.

The Moses Riddle

Moses was the son of the Pharaoh's daughter. He was also the daughter of the Pharaoh's son. How could this be?

Find clues on p. 60 and the answer on p. 82.

Cold Comfort

Why did a girl put her pet into the fridge?

Find clues on p. 60 and the answer on p. 82.

Hit Parade

A pop singer had three hits in the space of one month but he was not pleased. Why?

Find clues on p. 60 and the answer on p. 82.

Royal Colors

The queen wore white in 2006, yellow in 2007, red in 2008, and green in 2009. What for?

Find clues on p. 61 and the answer on p. 82.

The Spy's Secret

Enemy agents murder a spy. They search him for secret information but fail to find any, so they dump his body, which is later recovered by the police. His spymaster does not know where the spy has concealed the information, but after speaking to the police he deduces where it is. How?

Find clues on p. 61 and the answer on p. 83.

The Safety Paradox

A safety improvement was introduced into a popular sport in order to reduce injury. It has had the opposite effect but it is still retained. What is it?

Find clues on p. 61 and the answer on p. 83.

Accidental Delay

A tourist had an accident in his car. There was little damage and no one complained or reported the accident. However, as a result the tourist found that he could not fly home. Why not?

Find clues on p. 61 and the answer on p. 84.

The Need to Read

Why did a large group of enthusiastic readers gather on a dock in New York City?

Find clues on p. 62 and the answer on p. 84.

Message Received

Although they had never met (in person or otherwise), Jack received a signal from Jill and as a result she had to walk to work. Why?

Find clues on p. 62 and the answer on p. 84.

Hanging Out

Why did a woman take a load of very wet laundry down from her clothesline and replace it with perfectly dry clothing?

Find clues on p. 62 and the answer on p. 84.

Smokescreen

Why did a mean boss install two smoke detectors in the office?

Find clues on p. 62 and the answer on p. 84.

Dead Line

John had a serious accident. When he got out of the hospital he was given a new cell phone, but this caused his death. What happened?

Find clues on p. 62 and the answer on p. 84.

Which Is Which?

I have two train tickets in my pocket. One is for the outward journey and one for the return trip. Without looking, how can I know which is which?

Find clues on p. 63 and the answer on p.85.

The Faulty Phone

The pay phone at the university was out of order and the telephone company was very tardy about coming to fix it until one bright student had an idea; the phone was fixed the next day. What was his idea?

Find clues on p. 63 and the answer on p. 85.

Invest in the Best

A man invested in a new home supply company called the Hexagon Company and made a lot of money; his wife invested in a similar home supply company called the Pentagon Company and lost everything. Why?

Find clues on p. 63 and the answer on p. 85.

Less Mess

Why did the local crime rate fall when a famous actress moved into a street?

Find clues on p. 63 and the answer on p. 85.

Badge of Honor

Betty committed an offense and so Marie was given an award. What was it?

Find clues on p. 63 and the answer on p. 85.

Oddly Dangerous

What lethal thing do elevators, money, hospital beds, and restaurant menus have in common?

Find clues on p. 64 and the answer on p. 85.

Quit It

A woman tried to give up smoking but this caused her death. How come?

Find clues on p. 64 and the answer on p. 86.

Pesky Pigeons

A Swiss city had a problem with pigeons swarming all over its tourist sites. Tourists were asked not to feed the pigeons but this did not solve the problem. What humane solution was found?

Find clues on p. 64 and the answer on p. 86.

More Airport Visitors

For three months a man and a woman travel from their home to the nearest airport every morning and travel back home each evening. They do not work at the airport and never travel anywhere by plane. Why do they go there?

Find clues on p. 64 and the answer on p. 86.

Cap Guns

Why do some models of the Kalashnikov AK-47 include a bottle opener as part of the rifle?

Find clues on p. 64 and the answer on p. 86.

Tie-land

John reported for work at his new job where all the employees wore ties. He was wearing a necktie but his supervisor instructed him to take it off and replace it with a clip-on tie. Why?

Find clues on p. 65 and the answer on p. 86.

No Thanks

A disabled man was offered a good job by a reputable university. Why did he turn it down?

Find clues on p. 65 and the answer on p. 86.

The Ungrateful Hero

A soldier fighting in a war was awarded a medal for bravery. He angrily refused to accept it. Why?

Find clues on p. 65 and the answer on p. 87.

Misrepresented

Certain criminal groups have been around for a long time and still exist. They feature in many stories, true and fictional, and are often described carrying out an activity involving a piece of wood. However, there is no evidence whatsoever that this activity ever took place. Who are the people and what is the activity?

Find clues on p. 65 and the answer on p. 87.

Coffin Hoppin'

A burglar broke into a funeral parlor to see what he could steal. However, a cleaner arrived unexpectedly so the burglar had to hide. He jumped into an empty open coffin in the viewing room and played dead. How did the cleaner immediately know that he was not dead?

Find clues on p. 65 and the answer on p. 87.

The Miserly Caterer

A caterer decided to economize on his equipment to save money on expenses, but his plan ended up backfiring. Why?

Find clues on p. 66 and the answer on p. 88.

Dotty

Why do drive-in banks have Braille on their automatic teller machines?

Find clues on p. 66 and the answer on p. 88.

The Unhappy Golfer

A mediocre golfer dreamed all his life of scoring a hole in one. However, when he eventually did drive his tee shot into the hole, he was not pleased. Why?

Find clues on p. 66 and the answer on p. 88.

Completely Cured

A woman had something annoying her when she went to the doctor's; by the time she saw the doctor it had stopped. What was it?

Find clues on p. 66 and the answer on p. 88.

The Car That Slowed Him Down

A Russian scientist worked very hard and eventually accumulated enough money to buy a car. However, he soon found that his research output decreased. Why?

Find clues on p. 67 and the answer on p. 88.

Such a Mensch

How did Willy Müller make telephones more user-friendly for Orthodox Jews?

Find clues on p. 67 and the answer on p. 88.

Out of Gas

....

Hugo's life was saved because he ran out of gas. Why?

Find clues on p. 67 and the answer on p. 89.

Theory of Relativity

....

A group of friends discovered that a man they'd seen with his mother was actually older than she was. How can you explain this impossibility?

Find clues on p. 67 and the answer on p. 89.

The Suspect

A detective, investigating a burglary that had been reported one winter afternoon, called on the prime suspect (who lived alone) late the same evening and asked him to account for his movements. The suspect responded that he had not been out of the house all day long. How did the detective know he was lying?

Find clues on p. 68 and the answer on p. 89.

That's Gratitude for You

Two people were killed (and others were injured) by the ungrateful swine that they were trying to help. Why?

Find clues on p. 68 and the answer on p. 90.

Tea Set Surprise

Two-year-old Sarah was given a tea set as a present and her father was delighted to see her using it, and even joined her in a make-believe tea party, until his wife came home. Then what happened?

Find clues on p. 68 and the answer on p. 90.

The Great Potato Escape

The famous bank robber John Dillinger escaped from prison by using a potato. How?

Find clues on p. 68 and the answer on p. 90.

You'll Kick Yourself

Where can you go to see people with more than the average number of legs?

Find clues on p. 68 and the answer on p. 91.

Tossed Salad

Why did a woman throw a tomato over a wall?

Find clues on p. 69 and the answer on p. 91.

Smoking Can Kill You

The writer Saki died because of a cigarette. How?

Find clues on p. 69 and the answer on p. 92.

Not a Good Deed?

A man prevented many innocent people from going to jail, but his action was unpopular. Why?

Find clues on p. 69 and the answer on p. 92.

The Air Up There

A man leaves an ordinary air-filled balloon on the floor of a room. When he comes back he finds the balloon is touching the ceiling. How come?

Find clues on p. 69 and the answer on p. 92.

Lateral Thinking Animal Quiz

1. How do you put a giraffe into a refrigerator?

2. How do you put an elephant into a refrigerator?

3. The Lion King is hosting an animal conference. All the animals attend, except one. Which animal does not attend?

4. There is a wide river you must cross, but it is inhabited by crocodiles. How do you get across?

5. There is a very, very tall coconut tree. Underneath it there are four animals—a gorilla, an orangutan, a chimpanzee, and a koala bear. They decide to compete to see who is the fastest to get a banana off the tree. Who do you think will win?

6. Three monkeys sat under a tree. One of them decides he ought to climb the tree and get a banana. How many monkeys are left sitting under the tree?

7. If you were a fast runner, would you prefer it if a bear attacked you or a crocodile?

Find the answers on p. 93.

CLUES

Monkey Business
- He found a way to deter them.
- He did not use fences or obstacles.
- No other animals are involved.
- The monkeys loved the sweet orange fruits.

A Simple Question
- The question did not involve the person's identity or appearance.
- The policeman was looking for a particular form of stolen goods.
- Thieves can be unobservant about the things they steal.

The Job Doctor
- The doctor provides a physical treatment.
- The treatment removes an impediment to respectability and employment.

Wrong Note
- The trombone player was competent and conscientious.
- He deliberately played the note and immediately realized that it was wrong.
- Something happened between the last time he'd played the score and this time.

In and Out
- Ronald was free to get in or out of the car.
- He was a famous figure.
- Wherever he went, he was driven by someone.

Ex-straw-dinary

- He used the straw for a specific purpose but it was not to do with building, packing, animals, or covering the ground.
- He used it inside a building.
- He used it to perform a duty that was required on special occasions.

You Never Call

- Alexander Graham Bell was moved to invent the telephone because of other research that he had carried out.
- He got along well with his mother and sister and would have liked to speak to them.
- This has nothing to do with distance or availability of equipment.

Legless

- Ricky became very choosy.
- This puzzle is rather literal.
- The puzzle would not work if he had been called Richard.

Disgruntlement

- The workers were disgruntled because many other workers had been given the day off to join celebrations but they had not.
- They worked in financial services.
- This happened in New York.

Cut!

- The immigration officials thought he might be a terrorist.

- He was asked the purpose of his visit and gave an unintentionally ambiguous reply.

Flying Fish

- She threw the fish to her husband.

- He had bought the fish.

- He was unsuccessful in his hobby.

All the World's a Stage

- He did not use deceit, threats, or intimidation.

- He appeared on stage only in one particular play.

- He did not have a speaking role.

- None of the other actors in the play could have performed in the same capacity.

Street Number

- This was an official notice painted on the street.

- Many streets have this marking but he was seeing it in an unusual way.

- Some letters were concealed

A Strange Creature

- Think of this from a wordplay angle.

- The answer is a two-word phrase.

The Frame Game

- He did this for security purposes with all the valuable paintings in the museum.
- He made a small mark on the painting where it could not normally be seen.

The Dopes

- An investigative TV program found a way to get testable samples from the politicians.
- They offered them a chance to promote themselves and treated them as they would have treated any other guests on the program.

The Blooper

- He passed safely through security checks.
- He had disguised himself.
- He was spotted doing something that gave him away.

Note This

- We are talking about musical harmony and mechanical tension.

Picture Perfect

- The woman has no connection with the children in the photograph.
- She was not delivering the photograph to someone or someplace.
- She carried the photo with her as a deterrent.

Marked Man

- The man did something every day that caused him to make the marks on the days he wore this shirt.
- The other shirts all shared a feature that this shirt didn't.

The False Confession

- He made a perfectly rational decision.
- Several other people benefited from his decision.
- He was protecting the real murderer. He did not like the murderer and they were not related.
- We all have to die someday.

Overdressed

- He was indoors and very uncomfortable.
- He did not do it to change his appearance or as part of a bet or game.
- He did it to save money.

The Tattooed Man

- He was physically normal and there was no medical purpose to the tattoos.
- He planned to go somewhere where he would need them.
- The tattoos contained information that he needed.

The Knifing

- The masked man deliberately stabbed Sam. This was no accident.
- The man wore a mask over his face—but not to hide his identity.
- Prompt medical attention saved Sam's life.

Deceitful Action

- The District Attorney did it to mislead someone—but not John Jones.
- He knew that his e-mails were being intercepted by a third party.

Just Add Water

- The supply of clean water was intermittent. It was often off for long periods.
- People collected clean water when they could.

Who's at the Door?

- Marjorie works on weekdays, and her job is relevant.
- She chooses to knock for safety reasons.
- Ringing the bell could be dangerous.

Fire! What Fire?

- The people were given a clear warning but they did not believe it.
- They were in a place of entertainment.

Flightless

- The men were helping the war effort but they were a long way from the enemy.
- The plane was fully capable for making progress under its own power but the men pushed it—and many other planes.
- This has nothing to do with saving fuel, reducing noise, avoiding enemy detection, or pilot availability.

Lab of the Rising Sun
- The thing that was grown was not a disease, a virus, or anything malicious.
- The Japanese grew it in a marine laboratory.
- This involves a territorial dispute.

The Bunk Stunk
- He knew that it would make the bed smell terrible.
- He had slept in the bed before but he did not intend to sleep in it again.
- He was a criminal and he took this action to assist him in an illegal plan.

Stage Only
- No one has any reason to believe the play wouldn't make a successful movie.
- It is a whodunit—a murder mystery—by a famous author.

The Weaker Sex?
- This is something physical and part of the body.
- The items are not normally seen.
- Individual men and women do not need these items to survive but the human race does.

Airport Visitor
- The man stands in line at the check-in but he never checks in.
- He profits from his behavior.
- He is a criminal.

Ad Home and Abroad
- The visual story of the dirty socks being cleaned was misunderstood in the Middle East.
- The individual images were understood. The story was not.

The Quake Mistake
- Something unusual started many of the fires.
- The extra fires were not started by gas mains breaking, animals, explosions, sparks, or lava.
- Financial motivations are involved.

Flower Power
- He did not do it to gain her attention or to win her affection.
- However, he did want to get to know her better.
- He delivered the flowers to her place of work.

The Returning Father
- The father was not motivated by guilt or love or duty or curiosity.
- He returned for selfish reasons.
- He wanted something from his son.

The Artful Solution
- They found a way to display their graffiti messages.
- They did not use paint or ink.
- In fact, they didn't add anything to the walls at all.

The Rattler

- He was not murdered, or killed in an accident.

- He was a famous writer who became deranged, collapsed, and died. The thing that killed him was silent at the time but rattled later.

- The rattling manifested itself years later in a rather gruesome way.

A Weighty Problem

- The man worked in a grocery store.

- He identified a problem and came up with a solution.

- Millions of people use his invention.

The Fortunate Nephew

- Cedric didn't force his aunt to change the will, no did he interfere with the will in any way.

- Edna did not want to favor one nephew over the others.

- Cedric was the eldest of the three nephews.

Unnoticed

- There was no censorship or cover-up of the deaths of these two great literary figures.

- They died in November 1963.

The Stranded Man

- The man did not borrow or steal a vehicle.

- He made sure that someone with a vehicle would be traveling to his village.

- He did not do anything illegal or irresponsible (such as calling an ambulance or the fire department).

Death of a Presenter
- The woman contracted cancer from something she spent a lot of time near during her work.
- She breathed in something that proved to be very dangerous.
- Some of the other theater workers were affected; most were not.

Shoe Clue
- There was nothing unusual about the shoes she wore in real life, nor about her feet or general appearance.
- She had played a famous role.
- She was a villain in a James Bond film.

Don't Look Now
- With the blindfold on, she couldn't see where she was going.
- There were no other people helping her find her way.
- This was done as part of her job.

Flat Out
- He didn't give her the car she wanted.
- He gave her something she could use in the bathroom.

Initial Condition
- He was not setting out to deceive or mislead.
- He did this in order to track something.
- He valued his privacy.

Value for Money?

- The charity gives a sticky badge to each contributor.
- People wear the sticky badges to show that they have contributed to the charity.
- The poor quality badges do not stick so well.

Cracking the Code

- I used trial and error but not much—it didn't take more than six tries.
- I did not observe anyone opening the door, nor did I use any devices to spy on people opening the door, nor did I use any electronic devices to find the secret code.
- I looked carefully at the buttons.

The Moses Riddle

- It is the same man, Moses, in each of the statements.
- There is no sex change involved.
- The second sentence does not contradict the first.

Cold Comfort

- She did it to help the pet.
- The pet was neither in distress nor in immediate danger.
- The pet was a reptile.

Hit Parade

- The pop singer produced and performed some good songs that sold moderately well.
- He was disappointed that he only had three hits; he had hoped for many more.
- His fan base was older and didn't use the Internet much.

Royal Colors

- The queen wore the colors but did not select them herself; someone else made the choice for her.
- She had thousands of busy and devoted supporters.
- The color helped identify the queen and show how old she was.

The Spy's Secret

- The police didn't know where the information was hidden either.
- The spymaster asked the police to describe the body, the clothes, and what was found on the man.
- There was nothing unusual in the list of common items that the police gave.

The Safety Paradox

- The safety improvement helped reduce minor injuries to one part of the body but led to greater long-term damage.
- It involves a piece of protective equipment used in a contact sport.

Accidental Delay

- No one was injured in the accident. The police were not informed and there were no legal or medical repercussions.
- The tourist was in fine physical condition before and after the accident.
- He could probably have taken an flight within the country, but not the international one he intended to take.
- He hit an animal in the accident, and the animal survived.

The Need to Read
- They wanted to read something that could not arrive by plane or Internet.
- It would eventually be read by millions—but they wanted to be the first.

Message Received
- Jill had no intention of sending a signal to Jack.
- The signal was not a sign, a look, or a written or spoken message.
- Jill walked to work because her car was missing.

Hanging Out
- The woman is married, but her husband wasn't home at the time.
- He was able to see the clothesline, however.

Smokescreen
- The boss was very suspicious, and he worried that his employees were goofing off.
- Only one of the smoke detectors was real.

Dead Line
- A traffic accident had left John unable to walk.
- His death was due to another traffic accident.
- The phone was to blame but not because he was distracted by it.

Which Is Which?

- The two tickets are of exactly the same size, thickness, and material.

- I could not have felt the difference at the beginning of my journey but I can now.

The Faulty Phone

- The student found a way to give the telephone company a strong incentive to fix the phone.

- The problem with the phone was that calls could not be made, but a different problem was reported.

Invest in the Best

- Both companies made building materials.

- The company names described the products.

Less Mess

- The actress did not employ any security personnel.

- Criminals operating in the area found it in their best interest to go elsewhere.

Badge of Honor

- Marie had not helped in any way in the detection of Betty's offense or her apprehension.

- Marie's award was not for courage or civic duty. It was for a physical achievement.

- Marie had not expected the award, though she had made an effort to receive it.

Oddly Dangerous

- The lethal thing they have in common can also cause less serious ailments.

- Each of the items is commonly used or handled by many different people.

Quit It

- She wasn't still smoking cigarettes when she died.

- A doctor tried to help her give up the habit but she misunderstood his instructions.

Pesky Pigeons

- The pigeons were not killed, displaced, or driven away.

- Over a period of time the number of pigeons declined.

- The rule was changed and tourists were allowed to feed the pigeons.

More Airport Visitors

- They don't have a hobby or interest involving the airport.

- Financial considerations play a part in their decision, but the man and woman do not go to the airport for direct financial gain.

- They spend very little money at the airport and do not meet people they know there.

- They visit the airport in the winter.

Cap Guns

- Earlier designs of the gun didn't have the bottle opener.

- Because the bottle opener was added to the design, the guns became more reliable.

Tie-land
- All the ties worn by other employees were also clip-ons.
- The instructions were for his own safety.

No Thanks
- The man had a visible medical condition that affected the upper half of his body.
- The school was a well known American university, the position he was offered was one he'd been looking for, and the university's facilities had no drawbacks as far as he was concerned.
- He turned the job down when he heard the name of the university.

The Ungrateful Hero
- This happened in World War II.
- The soldier had been courageous and deserved a medal. He did not feel that he was unworthy of recognition.
- The medal was awarded by an ally.

Misrepresented
- These criminal groups are gangs of thieves, of a sort.
- Children often dress up as them.
- The activity with the piece of wood was supposedly a punishment that led to death.

Coffin Hoppin'
- The burglar lay silent and motionless.
- The cleaner could tell from a distance that the man was an intruder, because of his appearance.

The Miserly Caterer

- The caterer wanted to save money on forks, knives, and spoons.
- At first, the cheaper utensils worked perfectly well.

Dotty

- The banks do not expect that the Braille panels will be used at the drive-in banks.
- There is no legal requirement to feature Braille on the drive-in machines. The banks do it for economic reasons.

The Unhappy Golfer

- His ball did not cause any damage or hit anyone or anything.
- It's traditional to buy a round of drinks for your fellow golfers after hitting a hole in one, but this isn't what upset him.
- He wouldn't be expected to buy a round of drinks after what happened.

Completely Cured

- The woman was not ill.
- The thing that annoyed her would have stopped whether she'd gone to the doctor or not.
- She was not pleased that it had annoyed her and she was even less pleased when it stopped.

The Car that Slowed Him Down

- He now drove to work instead of taking public transport.
- He could get to work in the same time and his activity at work was unaffected.
- His creativity was reduced.

Such a Mensch

- Othodox Jews are forbidden from doing work on the Sabbath.
- Willy Müller invented a telephone accessory.

Out of Gas

- There are no tricky double meanings in the premise of the puzzle; Hugo's vehicle ran out of fuel.
- Running out of gas didn't cause him to avoid a collision. In fact, he was not traveling at the time.
- He was saved from a form of poisoning.

Theory of Relativity

- Many thousands of other people saw this man and his mother as well.
- The friends were surprised, but didn't find the situation unbelievable.
- Many of the things they had seen the man do did not actually happen.

The Suspect
- The answer does not involve tracks in the snow, or any other physical evidence left by the weather.
- There was no clue in the suspect's clothing or the items in the room.
- The detective noticed something to do with the suspect's pet.

That's Gratitude for You
- Their helpers were full of noble motives and wanted to free them from captivity.
- They rushed to freedom as soon as they could.

Tea Set Surprise
- The daughter served cups of water to herself and her father, pretending it was tea.
- Sarah's mother told her husband something that shocked him.

The Great Potato Escape
- Dillinger did not use the potato to hide something or as a method of communication.
- He modified the potato in some way.

You'll Kick Yourself
- You wouldn't necessarily need to go to a circus sideshow or a medical museum.
- Think about the meaning of the term "average."

Tossed Salad

- The wall was a prison wall.
- She was passing something to a confederate.
- The tomato was chosen to get around a security measure.

Smoking Can Kill You

- He did not die of a smoking-related illness or, indeed, any illness.
- Someone else smoked the cigarette.
- Saki died a violent death.

Not a Good Deed?

- The man was a world leader who had just come into power.
- The risk of going to jail was just one aspect of an activity of which he disapproved.
- He was a communist leader and the activity could be seen as promoting capitalism.

The Air Up There

- The air in the balloon had undergone no change.
- The balloon was floating near the ceiling when he returned.
- Something unfortunate had happened.

Lateral Thinking
Geography and Math Quiz

1. Which country has the longest border with France?

2. Which country's capital is the anagram of another country's name?

3. Where can you build a house with all four walls facing north?

4. Which U.S. states are the most northerly, most southerly, most westerly, and most easterly?

5. What country has the longest name that alternates consonants and vowels (e.g., Mexico or Canada)?

6. In what other country could you once have found the capital city of Norway?

7. Move one digit to make this equation correct:
   $62 - 63 = 1$

8. What number gets bigger the more you take away?

9. Consider numbers like FIVE, which when written in capital letters require only straight strokes of the pen. No positive integer can be written with the same number of strokes as the number itself, though TWENTY-NINE comes close, with 30 strokes (counting the hyphen). Can you write a mathematical expression, using only straight lines, that's equal to the number of lines used to write it?

Find the answers on p. 93.

ANSWERS

Monkey Business

He planted lemon trees all around the edge of the orange orchard. Once the monkeys tasted a few bitter lemons they left the orchard alone.

A Simple Question

The policeman was at a border crossing. He would stop a car, stare straight into the driver's eyes and ask, "What color is your vehicle?" If the car was stolen, the driver would often give himself away by looking around or hesitating.

The Job Doctor

The doctor removes tattoos.

Wrong Note

A spider had crawled onto the score the last time the musician played it, and gotten squashed when he closed it. When he reopened it the next time, he mistook the black spot that used to be the spider for a note.

In and Out

Ronald Reagan had been President of the United States for eight years. Whatever car he traveled in always had security clearance through all traffic, so the only time it ever stopped was when he arrived at his destination. When he was no longer in office, he was still driven everywhere, but the car stopped at traffic lights. When the car stopped his first reaction was to think that they had arrived.

Ex-straw-dinary

When a pope dies, the cardinals are closeted away until they elect a new pope. After each round of discussions, one of them sends a signal by setting fire to the ballots used to cast votes for the new pope. Historically, straw was added to the fire to generate dark smoke if there was no result so far. (Today, chemicals are used instead.) Once there is a conclusive result, only the ballot papers are used in the fire, producing white smoke, and the waiting crowds celebrate.

You Never Call

They were both profoundly deaf. Bell's researches into deafness and the workings of the ear led to the invention of the telephone.

Legless

Ricky lost the leg of the R and became picky.

Disgruntlement

On October 28, 1886, the Statue of Liberty was unveiled in New York. The day was declared a public holiday but banks and other financial institutions did not give employees the day off. Disgruntled workers joined in by throwing out of their office windows the spools of narrow paper on which stock prices were written. The spools unwound as they fell from the tall buildings and the tradition of the ticker tape parade was born.

Cut!

When asked what was the purpose of his visit, the movie director answered, "To shoot a pilot." He meant that he was going to make a trial episode of a new TV show, but the border officials misunderstood him.

Flying Fish

She's throwing the fish to a man who's had an unsuccessful fishing trip. He wants to be able to say truthfully that the fish he serves his guests for dinner is one he caught himself.

All the World's a Stage

He never got on stage during his lifetime. However, he left a large bequest to the theater on the condition that his skull be used in the play *Hamlet*.

Street Number

This was at a taxi stand, and the man was looking at the word TAXIS painted on the street, but seeing it from the wrong direction—upside down and back to front. The wheels of a taxi were covering the letters TA.

A Strange Creature

A manx cat (a type of cat with no tail) consists of a cross (the letter "x") between man and cat.

The Frame Game

The curator is adding inconspicuous identifying marks on a part of the painting hidden from view under the frame, as a safeguard against false claims and ransom demands. If someone claims to have the stolen painting, the curator can ask, "What is the number printed under the frame?" or he can check to quickly ascertain whether, if the painting is stolen and returned, the returned painting is a forgery.

The Dopes

A TV show offered to interview the politicians, who jumped at the chance of publicity. The makeup pads used on their foreheads absorbed beads of perspiration, which were analyzed to reveal traces of illegal drugs.

The Blooper

He dressed as a Muslim woman complete with veil. However, out of force of habit he went to the men's room rather than the women's, and was spotted.

Note This

In a string quartet, or the string section of an orchestra, where the instruments' strings must be extremely taut.

Picture Perfect

The woman gets out the photograph whenever she receives unwanted attention from men sitting next to her. She shows them the photograph as a way of deflecting their interest.

Marked Man

The man habitually kept a mechanical pencil in the pocket of his shirt. One of his shirts, however, had no pocket, so when he would unthinkingly try to put the pencil in his pocket, he would mark up the front of the shirt.

The False Confession

Bob was on death row, and due to be executed. Fred approached him with an offer. If Bob would agree to confess to a crime which Fred had committed, Fred would give Bob's family $500,000. Bob agreed.

Overdressed

At the airport, George found that he was over the luggage allowance and had to pay for the extra weight. So he took clothes out of his suitcase and wore them, since body weight and clothes worn were not charged extra.

The Tattooed Man

He wanted to help his brother break out of prison. He had a complicated tattoo put onto his body. It contained coded information and prison layout plans disguised as art. He committed a crime and was sent to prison. The tattoo was the best way to bring in all the information he needed. This was a plot point in the TV series *Prison Break*.

The Knifing

The masked man was a surgeon wearing a surgical mask in the operating theater. He saved Sam's life.

Deceitful Action

John Jones and Bill Smith were both charged with murder. Each denied the charge and each was represented by a different lawyer. The D.A. offered each man a deal—confess and incriminate the other for a reduced charge. Both men declined. The D.A. found out that Bill Smith and his lawyer were illegally tapping into the D.A.'s systems and reading confidential e-mails. The D.A. sent the bogus e-mail as a test. When Bill read that John Jones was about to do a deal and implicate him he decided that he should act first—so he accepted a deal by confessing and incriminated Jones.

Just Add Water

When the water supplies were cut off many people filled their baths with all the water they could from the tank or the water pipes. They left their faucets (taps) turned on to take all the water they could until it ran dry. Many forget to turn off their faucets. If they were out when the water was reconnected then they returned to find their homes flooded.

Who's at the Door?

Marjorie worked on weekdays as a gas leak detector. When someone phoned in a suspected gas leak she would visit their house to check for leaks. Gas leak inspectors never ring doorbells in case a spark causes an explosion.

Fire! What Fire?

The people were in a circus tent that was in danger of being consumed by a fire that they could not yet see. A clown came out to warn them but they just laughed, thinking it was a joke.

Flightless

In World War II, the U.S. wished to help Great Britain by giving or lending airplanes, but their neutrality (before Pearl Harbor) prevented them from doing so. Specifically, they were not allowed to hand over airplanes that had taken off in the U.S. and landed in Europe or the British Commonwealth. The planes flew to a flat field near the Canadian border where the crew pushed them across the border.

Lab of the Rising Sun

The Japanese grew coral in marine laboratories to build up a cluster of rocks into islands 1,000 miles south of Tokyo in the Pacific Ocean. By building up the rocks into coral islands the Japanese can confirm that the islands belong to them and stop Chinese military activity and exploration in the area. (China claims that since they are so small, they are rocks, not islands, and cannot be claimed as sovereign territory by Japan, and thus Japan can't prevent China from doing what it will with them.)

The Bunk Stunk

The man planned to escape from prison that evening. He knew that tracker dogs would be used to track him and that they normally took the fugitive's scent from the bed or his clothes. The manure disguised his scent. (Based on a scene from the TV series *Prison Break*.)

Stage Only

Agatha Christie in her will stated that her play, *The Mousetrap*, should not be filmed or adapted for TV until after it finished its run as a play in London. It went on to be the longest running play and so it was not filmed.

The Weaker Sex?

The smallest cell in the human body is the male sperm. The largest is the female ovum.

Airport Visitor

The man is a criminal who stands in line with other people at the airport check-in in order to read the luggage labels containing their home addresses. He and his friend then burgle their empty houses.

Ad Home and Abroad

The images were shown in a logical left to right arrangement on the poster. Arabs read right to left so they saw a story about a detergent that made clean socks dirty.

The Quake Mistake

Insurance companies did not give coverage for earthquakes in San Francisco but they did cover fire. Many people whose homes were damaged or destroyed by the earthquake deliberately set them alight so that they could make a claim on their insurance policies.

Flower Power

The man is a private investigator. He wants to trace a woman's movements, but doesn't know what she looks like. He does know her name and the large office at which she works, so he has the flowers delivered and waits to see which woman leaves the office at the end of the day with the bunch of flowers

The Returning Father

The father was very ill with a kidney disease and was hoping to get a kidney transplant from his only living blood relative, his son.

The Artful Solution

They used stencils and powerful detergents on dirty walls. Where the wall was cleaned it left their graffiti message, but since they had not applied any paint they were safe from prosecution.

The Rattler

Nobody is sure why the great gothic writer Edgar Allan Poe died so suddenly at the age of 40. But it is said that years later when his skull was shaken it rattled. This leads to the suspicion that a brain tumor caused his death. The brain then decomposed but the tumor shrunk into a hardened form and stayed there.

A Weighty Problem

The man worked in a supermarket and noticed that when shoppers' baskets became too heavy they stopped buying. So he invented the supermarket cart and as a result became very rich.

The Fortunate Nephew

When Edna made her will she had just one nephew, Cedric. She left all her money to him. Alec and Billy were born later and Edna died unexpectedly, not having updated her will.

Unnoticed

Lewis and Huxley died on the same day. Unfortunately for them it was the same day that President John F. Kennedy was shot in Dallas. The assassination dominated all the media.

The Stranded Man

With the money he had, he ordered a pizza to be delivered from the pizza parlor in his village. He then persuaded the deliveryman to give him a lift home on his scooter.

Death of a Presenter

The poor woman had died from inhaling asbestos from the old safety curtain in the theater, which was always lowered as she was presenting flowers.

Shoe Clue

Lotte Lenya played the evil Rosa Kleb in the 1963 James Bond film *From Russia With Love*. In the movie she wears shoes with poisoned switchblades with which she kicks and kills people.

Don't Look Now

She was training a guide dog.

Flat Out

The man's wife weighed 120 pounds, so he gave her a bathroom scale. It went from 0 to 120 in no time at all when she stepped on it!

Initial Condition

The man hates junk mail and uses the middle initial to track who's given his name away for mailing purposes. If he receives unwanted mail addressed to John C. Doe he knows who gave his name away and he complains to them.

Value for Money?

The charity gives sticky badges to each donor. The cheaper badges do not stick as well and fall off so donors will often make a second contribution for another badge.

Cracking the Code

Three of the buttons were very shiny, showing that they were commonly used. I just had to try six possible combinations of these three buttons to find the solution.

The Moses Riddle

Moses was the son of the Pharaoh's daughter. The second sentence is simply a restatement of the first. He was the Pharaoh's daughter's son. So he was the *daughter of the Pharaoh's* son.

Cold Comfort

The girl had a pet tortoise, which should hibernate in the winter. Mild weather had prevented the tortoise from going to sleep so she put it into the fridge to fool the tortoise into hibernating.

Hit Parade

The three hits were the only hits on his website.

Royal Colors

It is the color (actually a daub of paint) that beekeepers paint on a queen bee every year to tell them in what year she was hatched. There is a five-year cycle.

The Spy's Secret

The spy's controller knew that the spy did not smoke, but a packet of cigarettes was found on his body. He examined it and found the message inside one of the cigarettes.

The Safety Paradox

Boxing gloves were introduced to reduce cuts and injuries to hands and to soften the blows from punches. In bare knuckle fighting you could easily break your hand if you hit your opponent's skull so most blows were to the body. Boxing gloves allow more punches to the head and the cumulative effect of these blows results in many cases of brain damage and death among professional boxers. In 100 years of bare-knuckle fighting in the U.S. there was not a single ring fatality.

Accidental Delay

An English tourist in Australia drove into a kangaroo. He thought it would be funny to take a photo of the dead animal wearing his jacket and a tie. He dressed the kangaroo in the items. The kangaroo had only been stunned. It suddenly leapt up and hopped off wearing the man's jacket, which contained his wallet and passport.

The Need to Read

This happened in the 19th century. They were there to be the first in America to get hold of the next chapter of the latest Charles Dickens novel. He wrote many works as serials and released them a chapter at a time.

Message Received

Jill had a remote control key for her car. Jack was a thief with a receiver who intercepted and recorded the signal. He later used it to unlock and steal her car.

Hanging Out

The woman lives by the sea and her husband is a smuggler. Her washing is color-coded; certain colors mean "all clear" (there are no police around, so it is safe to come ashore). Other colors mean "danger." The police arrived suddenly so she had to hang out different clothes without any notice.

Smokescreen

One was a real smoke detector. The other was a camera disguised as a smoke detector so the boss could keep an eye on his employees.

Dead Line

After the accident, John used an electric wheelchair. The signal from his phone interfered with the controls of his wheelchair, sending him into the middle of a busy road.

Which Is Which?

My ticket for the outward journey has already been punched by the ticket inspector so I can feel the hole in it without looking.

The Faulty Phone

The student suggested that the telephone company be informed that due to a malfunction, students were able to make free international phone calls on that telephone, and had been doing so all day. The phone company was so worried about the loss of revenue that they sent engineers to fix it immediately.

Invest in the Best

The Hexagon Company made regular hexagonal tiles, which fit together perfectly and sold well. The Pentagon Company made regular pentagonal tiles, which can't fit together to tile a surface without gaps. These tiles sold poorly.

Less Mess

The many paparazzi photographers who would lie in wait for the actress deterred any burglars and muggers who had previously preyed on the area.

Badge of Honor

Betty won the gold medal at an Olympics event but was subsequently disqualified for using illegal drugs. Marie, who had finished fourth, was consequently awarded a bronze medal.

Oddly Dangerous

They are among the most common sources of bacteria, which cause fatal diseases.

Quit It

A doctor prescribed nicotine patches for her. Mistaking their purpose she rolled them up, lit them, and inhaled them. She died from nicotine poisoning.

Pesky Pigeons

The Swiss authorities gave out free bags of pigeon food to visitors. The food contained a contraceptive that did not harm the pigeons but prevented them from reproducing.

More Airport Visitors

The man and woman are retirees on a fixed income who cannot afford to heat their drafty house during the winter months. There is a free airport shuttle, so they go to the heated airport (which has an extensive shopping and dining concourse, and many places to sit), and stay there all day, and use a small space heater to warm their bedroom in the evening. They go to the airport every day until warmer weather returns.

Cap Guns

Soldiers were using the gunsight as a bottle opener, which could twist the sight. By incorporating a proper bottle opener into the rifle this misuse was eliminated.

Tie-land

John was hired as a prison guard. All the guards wore ties, but strictly clip-on ties because of the danger that a prisoner might grab a regular tie and use it to throttle its wearer.

No Thanks

He was a hunchback. His employment agency found him a position at Notre Dame University in Notre Dame, Indiana, but he did not want to be known as the hunchback of Notre Dame.

The Ungrateful Hero

In World War II, Finland fought alongside Germany on the Russian front. The Finns were not Fascist, just anti-Soviet. The Germans awarded an Iron Cross to a Jewish soldier fighting for the Finns. He rejected it.

Misrepresented

Pirates are often shown sending captives to their deaths by making them "walk the plank." There is no reliable evidence that this ever happened, yet it is ingrained into our image of pirates.

Coffin Hoppin'

The cleaner knew that the funeral director always dressed dead men in suits and ties before laying them in the coffins. The burglar was wearing casual clothes.

The Miserly Caterer

The caterer replaced all his metal cutlery with plastic cutlery. But when he tried to sterilize them for reuse, they all melted.

Dotty

Banks order automatic teller machines by the thousands and it is cheaper to have them all the same than to have a limited set for drive-in banks without the Braille.

The Unhappy Golfer

The golfer sliced his tee shot badly and it ended up rolling into the hole—but a different hole from the one he was playing. He had the embarrassment of collecting his ball from the wrong hole and replaying his shot with a penalty in front of his companions.

Completely Cured

The woman's wristwatch was annoying her, because it kept losing time. The watch stopped when its battery finally ran out as she was waiting in the lobby of her doctor's office.

The Car That Slowed Him Down

The Russian scientist had previously traveled to work on the train, which was where he'd had most of his best ideas. Now he had to concentrate on the dangerous traffic conditions as he drove to work and his source of creative ideas dried up.

Such a Mensch

In 1935 Willy Müller invented the first automatic telephone-answering machine. Orthodox Jews were not allowed to answer the telephone on the Sabbath so they previously missed many important calls.

Out of Gas

Hugo tried to commit suicide by sitting in his car with the engine running and a tube taking the exhaust fumes into the vehicle. He was saved when the gas ran out.

Theory of Relativity

They had watched the movie *North by Northwest*, in which Cary Grant plays the lead. He was one year older than Jessie Royce Landis, the actress who played his mother. (They could have had the same experience by watching Laurence Olivier in *Hamlet*, who was *twelve* years older than Eileen Herlie, the actress playing Gertrude, Hamlet's mother.)

The Suspect

As he entered the house the detective noticed that the suspect's cat was asleep on the hood of his car. On a cold evening, the cat would only lie there if it was warm, indicating that the car had been used.

That's Gratitude for You

Animal rights activists broke down a fence around a pig farm, freeing thousands of pigs awaiting slaughter. Two of the animal rights activists were trampled to death by the escaping pigs.

Tea Set Surprise

Sarah served her father "cups of tea" by pouring water from her teapot into a cup. Her father gladly went along and drank the tea. When his wife came home she pointed out that Sarah couldn't reach the sink, so the only place from which Sarah could get the water was the toilet!

The Great Potato Escape

On March 3, 1934, Dillinger escaped from the high security county jail at Crown Point, Indiana. He used a replica of a gun, carved from a potato and blackened with shoe polish.

You'll Kick Yourself

Anywhere. There are some people with no legs or one leg, so the average number of legs per person is very slightly less than two. Anyone with two legs has more than the average.

Tossed Salad

Dublin's Mountjoy Jail had a big drug problem. Drugs were getting into the jail by people hiding them in tennis balls and throwing the tennis balls over the wall. Then the authorities put huge nets over the open spaces of the jail to prevent this. The drug dealers then instead threw tomatoes with drugs inside. They caught in the net, but birds ate the fruit and the drugs fell through.

Smoking Can Kill You

Saki (the pen name of H.H. Munro) was a British officer in World War I. He was in a trench at night when one of his soldiers lit a match to light a cigarette. As Saki shouted "Put that bloody cigarette out," he was killed by a sniper's bullet.

Not a Good Deed?

When Fidel Castro became leader of Cuba, he banned the playing or sale of the game Monopoly, ordering all copies of the game to be destroyed.

The Air Up There

A pipe burst, flooding the room to a great depth. The balloon rose with the water.

Lateral Thinking Animal Quiz Answers

1. Open the refrigerator, put in the giraffe, and close the door.
2. Open the refrigerator, take out the giraffe, put in the elephant, and close the door.
3. The elephant. It is in the refrigerator.
4. You swim across. All the crocodiles are attending the animal conference.
5. None of them. You cannot get a banana off a coconut tree.
6. Three. It takes more than a decision to change anything.
7. You would much prefer it if the bear attacked the crocodile and not you.

Lateral Thinking Geography and Math Quiz Answers

1. Brazil. French Guyana is considered to be part of France and it has a huge border with Brazil.
2. Lima, the capital of Peru, is an anagram of Mali.
3. At the South Pole.
4. Alaska, Hawaii, Alaska, and Alaska. The reason Alaska is both the most westerly and most easterly is because some of its islands lie over the 0° line of longitude and are therefore east of the U.S.
5. United Arab Emirates.
6. Czechoslovakia contains the word Oslo, though the country no longer exists. (In 1993 it split into the Czech Republic and Slovakia.)
7. $2^6 - 63 = 1$
8. SIX becomes IX and then X (9 and 10 in Roman numerals)
9. Multiple solutions are possible, but TEN + TEN, written with 20 strokes, is the simplest.

INDEX

Accidental Delay, 32
  clues, 61
  answer, 84
Ad Home and Abroad, 24
  clues, 57
  answer, 79
Air Up There, 47
  clues, 69
  answer, 92
Airport Visitor, 24
  clues, 56
  answer, 79
All the World's a Stage, 16
  clues, 52
  answer, 73
Artful Solution, The, 26
  clues, 57
  answer, 80

Badge of Honor, 36
  clues, 63
  answer, 85
Blooper, The, 17
  clues, 53
  answer, 74
Bunk Stunk, The, 23
  clues, 56
  answer, 78

Cap Guns, 39
  clues, 64
  answer, 87
Car That Slowed Him
  Down, The, 43
  clues, 67
  answer, 88
Coffin Hoppin', 40
  clues, 65
  answer, 87
Cold Comfort, 31
  clues, 60
  answer, 82
Completely Cured, 42
  clues, 66
  answer, 88
Cracking the Code, 30
  clues, 60
  answer, 82
Cut!, 15
  clues, 52
  answer, 73

Dead Line, 35
  clues, 62
  answer, 84
Death of a Presenter, 28
  clues, 59
  answer, 81
Deceitful Action, 21
  clues, 55
  answer, 76
Disgruntlement, 15
  clues, 51
  answer, 73
Dopes, The, 17
  clues, 53
  answer, 74
Don't Look Now, 29
  clues, 59
  answer, 81
Dotty, 41
  clues, 66
  answer, 88

Ex-straw-dinary, 14
  clues, 51
  answer, 72

False Confession,196
  clues, 54
  answer, 76
Faulty Phone, The, 35
  clues, 63
  answer, 85
Fire! What Fire?, 22
  clues, 55
  answer, 77
Flat Out, 30
  clues, 59
  answer, 81
Flightless, 23
  clues, 55
  answer, 78
Flower Power, 25
  clues, 57
  answer, 79
Flying Fish, 15
  clues, 52
  answer, 73
Fortunate Nephew, The,
  32
  clues, 58
  answer, 81

Frame Game, The, 17
  clues, 53
  answer, 74
Great Potato Escape, The,
  45
  clues, 68
  answer, 90
Hanging Out, 34
  clues, 62
  answer, 84
Hit Parade, 31
  clues, 60
  answer, 82
In and Out, 14
  clues, 50
  answer, 72
Initial Condition, 30
  clues, 59
  answer, 82
Invest in the Best, 35
  clues, 63
  answer, 85
Job Doctor, The, 13
  clues, 50
  answer, 72
Just Add Water, 21
  clues, 55
  answer, 77
Knifing, The, 20
  clues, 54
  answer, 76
Legless, 15
  clues, 51
  answer, 73
Lab of the Rising Sun, 23
  clues, 56
  answer, 78
Lateral Thinking Animal
  Quiz, 48
  answer, 93
Lateral Thinking
  Geography and Math
  Quiz, 70
  answer, 93
Less Mess, 36
  clues, 63
  answer, 85

Marked Man, 18
    clues, 54
    answer, 75
Message Received, 33
    clues, 62
    answer, 84
Miserly Caterer, The, 41
    clues, 66
    answer, 88
Misrepresented, 40
    clues, 65
    answer, 87
Monkey Business, 12
    clues, 50
    answer, 72
More Airport Visitors, 38
    clues, 64
    answer, 86
Moses Riddle, The, 31
    clues, 60
    answer, 82

Need to Read, The, 33
    clues, 62
    answer, 84
No Thanks, 40
    clues, 65
    answer, 87
Not a Good Deed?, 47
    clues, 69
    answer, 92
Note This, 17
    clues, 53
    answer, 74

Oddly Dangerous, 37
    clues, 64
    answer, 85
Out of Gas, 44
    clues, 67
    answer, 89
Overdressed, 19
    clues, 54
    answer, 76

Pesky Pigeons, 38
    clues, 64
    answer, 86
Picture Perfect, 18
    clues, 53
    answer, 75

Quake Mistake, The, 25
    clues, 57
    answer, 79

Quit It, 37
    clues, 64
    Answer, 86

Rattler, The, 27
    clues, 58
    answer, 80
Returning Father, The, 26
    clues, 57
    answer, 79
Royal Colors, 32
    clues, 61
    answer, 82

Safety Paradox, The, 32
    clues, 61
    answer, 83
Shoe Clue, 29
    clues, 59
    answer, 81
Simple Question, A, 12
    clues, 50
    answer, 72
Smokescreen, 34
    clues, 62
    answer, 84
Smoking Can Kill You, 47
    clues, 69
    answer, 92
Spy's Secret, The, 32
    clues, 61
    answer, 82
Stage Only, 23
    clues, 56
    answer, 78
Stranded Man, The, 28
    clues, 58
    answer, 81
Strange Creature, A, 47
    clues, 52
    answer, 74
Street Number, 16
    clues, 52
    answer, 74
Such a Mensch, 43
    clues, 67
    answer, 88
Suspect, The, 45
    clues, 68
    answer, 89

Tattooed Man, The, 20
    clues, 54
    answer, 76

Tea Set Surprise, 45
    clues, 68
    answer, 90
That's Gratitude for You,
    45
    clues, 68
    answer, 90
Theory of Relativity, 44
    clues, 67
    answer, 89
Tie-land, 39
    clues, 65
    answer, 87
Tossed Salad, 46
    clues, 69
    answer, 91

Ungrateful Hero, The, 40
    clues, 65
    answer, 87
Unhappy Golfer, The, 42
    clues, 66
    answer, 88
Unnoticed, 32
    clues, 58
    answer, 81

Value for Money?, 30
    clues, 60
    answer, 82

Weaker Sex?, The, 23
    clues, 56
    answer, 79
Weighty Problem, A, 27
    clues, 58
    answer, 80
Which Is Which?, 34
    clues, 63
    answer, 85
Who's at the Door?, 22
    clues, 55
    answer, 77
Wrong Note, 13
    clues, 50
    answer, 72

You Never Call, 15
    clues, 51
    answer, 73
You'll Kick Yourself, 46
    clues, 68
    answer, 91

About the Authors

Paul Sloane lives in Camberley, Surrey, England. He has been an avid collector and composer of lateral thinking puzzles for many years. He runs the Lateral Puzzles Forum on the Internet, where readers are able to pose and solve puzzles interactively: **www.lateralpuzzles.com.**

Sloane has his own business helping organizations use lateral thinking to find creative solutions and improve innovation. The Web site is: **www.destination-innovation.com.**

He is a renowned speaker and course leader. He is married with three daughters, and in his spare time he plays golf, chess, and tennis.

Des MacHale was born in County Mayo, Ireland. He lives in Cork with his wife, Anne, and they have five children. He is Emeritus Professor of Mathematics at University College Cork, where he taught for nearly 40 years. He has a passionate interest in humor and puzzles of all sorts and has written over sixty books on various subjects—lateral thinking puzzles, jokes, a biography of George Boole, three on John Ford's film *The Quiet Man*, and a ten-volume *Wit* series of humorous quotations. He is a regular contributor of puzzles to the Brainteaser section of *The Sunday Times* of London and frequently appears on TV and radio.

MacHale's other interests include bird-watching (ah, so relaxing), classical music and Irish traditional music, book collecting, photography, old movies, quizzes, words, and humor. He is interested in virtually everything except wine, jazz, and reality TV shows.

Paul Sloane and Des MacHale are the authors of more than a dozen lateral thinking puzzle books. More recent titles include *Colorful Lateral Thinking Puzzles, Great Lateral Thinking Puzzles, Hall of Fame Lateral Thinking Puzzles, Kick Yourself Puzzles,* and *Lethal Lateral Thinking Puzzles.*